Traverse Theatre Company

Crash
by Andy Duffy

Performed at the Traverse Theatre, 7 - 30 August 2015

A Traverse Theatre Company Commission

Crash
by Andy Duffy

Cast

Jamie Michie

Creative

Director	Emma Callander
Assistant Director	Sunniva Ramsay
Production Manager	Kevin McCallum
Company Stage Manager	Gemma Turner
Deputy Stage Manager	Naomi Stalker
Costume Supervisor	Kat Smith
Additional Music by	Andy Cowan

Company Biographies

Emma Callander (Director)

Emma is an Associate Artist, and former Associate Director of the Traverse Theatre. Directing credits at the Traverse include: *The Day the Pope Emptied Croy* by Martin McCormick, *Crash* by Andy Duffy, *Mrs. Barbour's Daughters* by AJ Taudevin and *The Queen of Lucky People* by Iain Heggie. Other directing credits include *Cuckooed* by Mark Thomas (winner of the Fringe First and Amnesty International Freedom of Speech Awards 2014), *Dalgety* by David Greig and *Supply* by Cathy Forde (A Play, A Pie and A Pint, Oran Mor), *Banksy: The Room in the Elephant* by Tom Wainwright (A Play, A Pie and A Pint, Oran Mor, Tobacco Factory Theatres, Arcola Theatre and national tour), and the *Arcadia Spectacular* for Glastonbury Festival. Emma is also Co-Artistic Director of Theatre Uncut and has directed the company's work at the Young Vic, Bristol Old Vic, The Arches Glasgow, Latitude Festival and the Traverse, where they were winners of the Herald Angel and Fringe First Awards for two years running.

Andy Duffy (Playwright)

Andy is a Glasgow-based writer. His first play *Nasty, Brutish and Short* was performed as part of the National Theatre of Scotland and Traverse Theatre *debuts* season at the Traverse Theatre in November 2008, and was directed by Dominic Hill. Other writing credits include *Waterproof*, which appeared at A Play, A Pie and A Pint, Oran Mor in 2009 and was later toured by Mull Theatre in 2012. Andy also contributed to *Gordon Brown: A Life In Theatre* which was curated by David Greig at the Traverse Theatre in May 2010.

Jamie Michie (Actor)

Jamie is a native Scotsman and consummate screen and stage actor. Feature film credits include *In The Heart Of The Sea* (Ron Howard), *The Selfish Giant* (Clio Barnard), *Route Irish* (Ken Loach), *Chavez* (Diego Luna), *Hector* (Jake Gavin) and *Sunset Song* (Terence Davies). For television,

Jamie played Steelshanks in Season 3 of HBO's juggernaut success *Game of Thrones*. Other recent TV projects include *Shetland 3*, *Humans*, *Chickens*, *Top Boy 2*, *Vera*, *Midsomer Murders* and *Skins*.

Jamie is delighted to be returning to the stage this summer with *Crash*.

Sunniva Ramsay (Assistant Director)

Sunniva Ramsay is Engagement Co-ordinator at the Traverse Theatre. She graduated in 2011 from the University of Glasgow with a First Class Honours MA in Theatre Studies. Prior to taking up post at the Traverse, Sunniva worked as an engagement artist, facilitator and director in venues including The Arches (Glasgow), The Royal Lyceum Theatre (Edinburgh) and North Edinburgh Arts.

Sunniva's directing credits include *A Cross, Rules of the Playground* (Lyceum Youth Theatre), *Scribble Showcase* (Traverse Theatre/Lyceum Youth Theatre). Assistant director credits include *Love With A Capital L, The Last Bloom* (A Play, A Pie and A Pint, Oran Mor), *A Taste Of …* and *Seven Billion Others and Me* (Lyceum Youth Theatre). Within her role as Traverse Engagement Co-ordinator, Sunniva regularly works as a dramaturg and workshop leader for emerging writers' programmes, including Scribble and Traverse Young Writers.

Crash was first produced as part of A Play, A Pie and A Pint, Autumn 2014.

Traverse Theatre Company

"One of the most exciting places for theatre in the UK."
The Guardian

The Traverse is Scotland's foremost theatre company dedicated to new writing.

Founded by a group of passionate arts enthusiasts seeking to extend the spirit of the Festival throughout the year, the Traverse Theatre Club opened in a former brothel in Edinburgh's Lawnmarket in 1963. Now, more than a half century on, the Traverse is an established part of Scotland's arts infrastructure, yet retains that essence of innovation and excitement. It remains committed to the original spirit of its founders, and to presenting audiences with a good story, well told. Under Artistic Director Orla O'Loughlin it continues to produce vibrant theatre for, and of, our time, further building its reputation with award-winning productions such as *The Artist Man and the Mother Woman, Quiz Show, Ciara* and *Spoiling.*

Internationally acclaimed as a powerhouse of new writing, the Traverse has launched the careers of some of Scotland's most celebrated writers, including John Byrne, David Greig, Gregory Burke, David Harrower, Liz Lochhead and Zinnie Harris. Many of today's finest actors have appeared on its stages, including Tilda Swinton, Billy Connolly, Robbie Coltrane, Bill Nighy and Alan Cumming.

The Traverse's impact is truly international: it frequently tours overseas, engages in artistic exchanges and partnerships – most recently in Québec, Turkey and South Korea – and, every August, it holds an iconic status as the theatrical heart of the Edinburgh Festival Fringe.

Always looking to the future, the Traverse leads Participation and Engagement programmes that engage with emerging writers and artistic talent to develop the next generation of theatre-makers.

Special Thanks

The work of the Traverse Theatre would not be possible without the support of:

ALBA | CHRUTHACHAIL

The Traverse extends grateful thanks to the many individuals, organisations, trusts and foundations that support and contribute to the theatre's work. Each plays an important part in securing the Traverse's future and maintaining its reputation as one of the world's most exciting theatres.

With special thanks to Katie Bradford, Iain Millar and Bridget Stevens.

Traverse Productions are generously supported by Cotterell & Co and Paterson SA Hairdressing.

Connect with us:

TravCast:

Find our monthly podcasts on **soundcloud.com** and **traverse.co.uk** with insights into the making of shows and featuring interviews with some of the UK's leading writers.

Traverse Theatre

The Company

Fiona Campbell	Box Office Manager
Jessica Chalmers	Box Office Senior Supervisor
Linda Crooks	Executive Producer & Joint Chief Executive
Claire Doohan	Marketing & Campaigns Officer
Claire Elliot	Deputy Electrician
Kisha Gallagher	Trading Company Manager
Ellen Gledhill	Development Manager
Tom Grayson	Deputy Box Office Manager
Rose Gregory	Trading Company Assistant Manager
Zinnie Harris	Associate Director
Rosie Kellagher	Literary Associate
Jonathan Kennedy	Technical Theatre Apprentice
Rebecca Leary	Receptionist/Administrator
Kath Lowe	Front of House Manager
Catherine Makin	Artistic Administrator
Francisca Martinez Garcia	Senior Kitchen Supervisor
Kevin McCallum	Head of Production
Bradley McCathie	Traverse Trading Senior Supervisor
Ruth McEwan	Assistant Producer
Ann Monfries	Head of Marketing & Sales
Ondine Oberlin	Box Office Supervisor
Orla O'Loughlin	Artistic Director & Joint Chief Executive
Cian O'Siochain	Press and Media Officer
Joy Parkinson	Marketing & Communications Assistant

Julie Pigott	Head of Finance & Administration
David Pollock	Operations Manager
Pauleen Rafferty	Payroll & HR Manager
Sunniva Ramsay	Engagement Co-ordinator
Renny Robertson	Chief Electrician
Michelle Sandham	Finance Officer
Tom Saunders	Lighting & Sound Technician
Gary Staerck	Head of Stage

Also working for the Traverse

Eleanor Agnew, Charlotte Anderson, Lindsay Anderson, Calum Brittain, Emma Campbell, Ben Clifford, Amy Cloonan, Hannah Cornish, Rachel Cullen, Koralia Daskalaki, Jonathan Dawson, Caitlin Delves, Euan Dickson, Judith Dobie, Uxia Dominguez Rial, Christine Dove, Rachel Duke, Calum Dwyer, Katherine Eggleston, Sarah Farrell, Daniel Findlay-Carroll, SorchaFitzgerald, Andrew Gannon, Anthony Gowling, Laura Grantham, Megan Hampton, Charles Hanks, Laura Hawkins, David Howie, Jennifer Hulse, Adam James, Miguel Leonisio Torrejon, Lynsey MacKenzie, Alan Massie, Cristina Matthews, Cleo McCabe, Kieran McCruden, Kirsty McIntyre, Edwin Milne, Alasdair Mitchell, Stephen Moir, Hal Morrissey Gillman, Liam Pike, Anna Reid, Simon Rutherford, Theodora Sakellaridou, Kolbrun Sigfusdottir, Rosalind Sim, Kathryn Smith, Olivia Stoddart, Joanne Sykes, Emma Taylor, Hannah Ustun, Jessica Ward, Rosemary Ward

Foreword from Director Emma Callander

Crash had me gripped from the moment I began to read it. The play landed on my desk through Open Submissions at the Traverse Theatre and I instantly knew we had come across an important story told by a unique Scottish voice. Andy Duffy has created a fascinating and disturbing character who challenges our sense of empathy right up until the final words he speaks. Is this a man suffering from insurmountable guilt, heightened by the extreme pressures of working in the financial market, or is he so emotionally detached that he has lost all sense of humanity? In the telling of such a deeply intimate story the play also raises complex questions around the morality of capitalism and the philosophy of human existence within the free market. In the continuing wake of the 2008 financial crisis, stories of culpability in the banking industry still fill our newspapers daily. *Crash* offers a provocative insight into an individual experience which challenges us to identify where we sit within the wider debate on where the ultimate responsibility lies.

Thanks to:
Susannah Armitage, Patrick McGurn, Andy Cowan and all on the *A Play, A Pie and A Pint* Oran Mor team, Orla O'Loughlin, Linda Crooks, Ruth McEwan, Catherine Makin, Andy McNamee, Sunniva Ramsay and the team at the Traverse and Jamie Michie for saying yes.

Foreword from Writer Andy Duffy

The car crash and the acts of violence came first. Deciding the main character was a trader came later. The stock market has fascinated me for the past six or seven years. I can't quite claim to have read every book ever written on the subject, but I felt I knew enough to talk about it in a play. Once the character was a trader, starting with a car crash and ending with the financial crash seemed obvious.

Crash is not an attempt to educate anyone about the markets. Theatre isn't a good medium for that anyway. If you're interested in the last financial crash there are plenty of good books about it, some by Nobel Prize-winning economists. It's a huge, complicated, generally compelling but occasionally tedious subject. You can skim the boring parts in a book. Plays, in performance at least, you have to sit through.

I'm aware there's another play I could have written. In this other play trading is shown to instil discipline, self-awareness and emotional fortitude, and leads people to a life of financial freedom. I'd still like to write that play at some point. Demonising those who work in the financial sector is too easy.

I'd like to thank Emma Callander, Jamie Michie, Susannah Armitage, Gary McNair, Alan McKendrick, and everyone at the Traverse and Oran Mor involved in the production.

CRASH

Andy Duffy

CRASH

OBERON BOOKS
LONDON

WWW.OBERONBOOKS.COM

First published in 2015 by Oberon Books Ltd
521 Caledonian Road, London N7 9RH
Tel: +44 (0) 20 7607 3637 / Fax: +44 (0) 20 7607 3629
e-mail: info@oberonbooks.com
www.oberonbooks.com

PB ISBN: 978-1-78319-953-2
E ISBN: 978-1-78319-954-9

Cover design by Emma Quinn

Printed, bound and converted
by CPI Group (UK) Ltd, Croydon, CR0 4YY.

Visit www.oberonbooks.com to read more about all our books
and to buy them. You will also find features, author interviews and
news of any author events, and you can sign up for e-newsletters
so that you're always first to hear about our new releases.

You wouldn't know it was there unless you were looking for it

When I go in there are a few people milling around in the hall

One or two business types

They're wearing suits anyway, I'm assuming that's what they are

Everyone looks pretty normal, though you never can tell I suppose

We go into a room, and after a few minutes the guy running the class comes in

He introduces himself, says his name is Toby

Which isn't a great name for a spiritual instructor

He asks us to take off our shoes, and sit on the mats provided

He says he's going to talk for a bit, then teach us a couple of simple meditation techniques

He congratulates everyone on taking this first step, which he hopes will start us on a lifelong practice of our own

Some hope

I take a look around the room

It's a fair size

The overheads on this place must be killing him

There's what, maybe thirty or so people here

Fifteen pounds a skull

How many classes could he take in a day?

It's barely a living wage

We need to calm the mind, he says

When we calm the mind we begin to see the world as it really is

We begin to see the truth

And the truth is, everything that happens, is created by us

But we can't see this basic truth

He looks round everyone in the room as he's talking

I notice an ad on the wall for a Buddhist retreat on the Isle of Skye

Allison always wanted to go to Skye but we never seemed to get around to it

We blame others, he says

Our parents, our partner, the government

Nothing ever happened you didn't allow to happen

He's looking straight at me when he says you

Take responsibility, he says

When he's done speaking he has us meditate for a bit

Sit in a comfortable position

Cross-legged, you don't need to if you can't manage it he says

Close your eyes or keep them open, it's up to you

We're going to concentrate on the breath

Either at the stomach or the nostrils

As you breathe in, you think *(Breathes in.)* this is an in breath

As you breathe out, *(Breathes out.)* this is an out breath

And that's it, that's all you do

Concentrate like your life depends on it, he says

It's not as easy as it sounds

After a while all I can think about is how much my legs are aching

Maybe I'm getting old

When we're done with that we move on to another technique

This time we're going to do a mantra

Which we'll repeat aloud

The words themselves don't mean anything

The purpose of the mantra is to free the mind of conscious thought

The mantra is, ah-lum-<u>bar</u>-dee-dum, ah-lum-<u>baa</u>-dee-dum

We repeat it after him

Ah-lum-<u>bar</u>-dee-dum, ah-lum-<u>baa</u>-dee-dum

Ah-lum-<u>bar</u>-dee-dum, ah-lum-<u>baa</u>-dee-dum

Ah-lum-<u>bar</u>-dee-dum, ah-lum-<u>baa</u>-dee-dum

Ah-lum-<u>bar</u>-dee-dum –

(Beat.)

Becoming enlightened feels a lot like making a prick of
yourself

——

In the office the next day I'm flicking through the papers
before the open when something catches my eye

It's a picture of this middle-aged woman, for some
reason she looks familiar

The article says she was stabbed thirteen times in the
chest, arms and back, in her own home

Police believe it was a robbery and she interrupted them
in the act

I look at the picture again, and I realise where I've seen
her before

She lives down the street from me – lived – down the
street from me

I think Allison, she might have spoken to her a couple of
times

I didn't know her at all

So, I think, how can she have created that situation?

How could she be responsible?

Maybe on another night she doesn't wake up –

But then that's not really under her control is it?

Or she realises there's someone downstairs but decides
to lock herself in her bedroom

So she just gets burgled, not killed

Or she buys a better alarm, or she moves home

Maybe living in a big house in a nice area was it

She was rich

She was asking for it

——

I find myself back at the class the following week

Same format, he talks for a bit, we meditate

'Your life is governed by fear', he says

I think, 'fucking tell me something I don't know'

'Fear of not getting what you want', he says

'Fear of getting it. Fear of losing it'

'What is it that you want?'

' … And what if you had everything you ever wanted?'

'What do you do then?'

When we come to say the mantra aloud this time he asks for a volunteer to lead it, someone from the group

A few hands go up, he picks out the woman in front of me, and introduces her as Kate

I think I saw her here last week but I'm not certain

I guess I didn't really notice her, but now I wonder why I didn't

She has long blonde hair and a lovely arse

Toby asks her to stand at the head of the class and kick it off whenever she's ready

She looks a bit uncomfortable but she tries to hide it with a smile

When she says the mantra there's a kind of innocence in the way she does it

I think about her on the drive home

When I see her there the following week I ask her if she'd like to go for a drink

She says yes

We go out a few times

She tells me she works in a book shop

She loves books

Which is handy if you work in a book shop, I suppose

She says she used to want to be a novelist, but she didn't have any talent for it

Not sure what talent has to do with anything

I hate novels, but she doesn't seem to mind

I think the only person who could write a novel is someone who really loves the sound of their own voice

At least poets have the good manners to keep their stuff short

I try to explain to her what I do but she looks a bit…

She does seem more interested when she finds out how much money I make

Although she did say, Oh, I've never had any interest in
money

Not sure I believe her to be honest

Money's power and freedom

Who's not interested in that?

In truth I think it excites her

It does most people

I guess I talk to her about Allison

How long we'd been married

Things like that

I tell her how things have been at work

The problems I've been having

She says to me, can't you just set out on your own?

I try to explain to her the level of risk involved, and why
it's a bad idea

In the process she convinces me it's not

'What is it you're afraid of?' she says

She seems to have this idea I'm some kind of…
I don't know

That I'm a better person than I really am

We move in together

Or rather, she moves in with me

She brings half a library with her but I've plenty of space

It was just me and Allison

The house is too big for two people really

It's too big for one anyway

It takes a bit of adjusting, but it is nice to have someone around

Although I spend more time hanging curtains than I would like

I think she likes coming home to me

She couldn't get a dog because of her allergies, I guess I'm the next best thing

She has a lightness about her

She laughs easily

So nothing seems a big deal

I start to think she might be an angel sent to save me

I know that sounds stupid

I said to her one time I thought every man who saw her wanted her, and they wanted to kill me and take my place

But she just laughed and told me to stop being such a mental bastard

Which is fair comment, I suppose

I would prefer it if she dressed down a bit, though

I don't want other men thinking about her body

A burkha would be ideal

I decide not to suggest it

—

John seems surprised when I tell him I'm leaving

It's all pretty amicable though

At least until the subject of my bonus comes up, which they want me to forfeit

Even though it's in my contract

It's not even about the money

Although it is a lot

And it's money I need

I call my lawyer and start proceedings against them as soon as I've left the building

I want them to give me what I'm due

I've worked with John for years

I don't expect anything from him

He's protecting his own interests

The same as anyone would

As I'm leaving he says something I find a bit odd

He says, if you don't know who you are, the market is an expensive place to find out

—

I spend the next few weeks getting things in place for my new fund

Registering for tax in the Cayman Islands and the like

I manage to secure a brokerage account with Meryl,
and in return for my business they allow me to give a
presentation at their offices to prospective clients

I give a talk to about twenty or so very wealthy
individuals and seeder fund managers about how the
equity markets have been going straight up for five years
so all the people running funds are uber-bulls and all
of the bears are currently out of work. And how this
is exactly the kind of situation where, when things go
south, all these managers run around saying, how could
this happen? Nobody could possibly have seen this
coming and so on

I show them my track record

They're impressed

Why wouldn't they be?

I'm enjoying myself

It's good to know you're good at something

I detail exactly how I intend to trade

In truth, it's mostly bullshit

I have no idea how I'll trade

It's just instinct, intuition, on any given trade on any
given day

But you can't tell that to these guys and expect them to
give you their money

I'm starting to realise the enormity of what I've taken on

How much I'll be responsible for

And if it fails…there's no one to blame but me

—

I guess things are pretty good with Kate

She says she's never been happier

I feel a bit less foolish chanting with her beside me

We've started doing Tai Chi together

If I don't get enlightened I'll at least get more limber

We talk about the meditation classes quite a lot

She's given me this huge pile of books to read

She said her manager, Gerald, had originally given them
to her

And that they'd changed her life

Some look interesting

Some are horseshit

Kate can't seem to tell the difference

They're called things like, *A Course in Miracles* and *The
Power of Now*

She even found one for me called, *Trading, a spiritual
journey*

It's written by an American, which puts me off a bit to be
honest

Not that I have anything against Americans

But they seem to think everything is a spiritual journey

We're having dinner with Gerald

She told me weeks ago

'It's on the calendar in the kitchen if you want to check'

She's been keen for me to meet him

Can't say I feel the same

She already talks about him more than I would like

When we arrive at the restaurant he's already there

He's younger than I thought he'd be

I never thought to ask her how old he is

He looks like a Gerald

During the meal he talks mostly about books

About writers I've never heard of

He says telling stories is what makes us human

A way of making sense of the world

Which sounds pretty sensible, but I'm in no mood to agree with him

Not after a couple of drinks

He spends half the night staring longingly at Kate

Although she thinks I imagine these things

I'd really love to give him a slap

Towards the end of the meal he brings up the subject of money

I get the impression this is the real reason we're all here

Says he wants to open another shop

A lease in an ideal location has become available, but he needs funds for refurbishment and he'll be running it at a loss for maybe a year or so and he's been to every bank and no one's interested in helping him out

He pauses

I guess he wants me to say something

Does he expect me to front him for it?

Maybe he wants me to take out half a mil in used fivers

Dump them on his plate and say, 'there you go mate. Go buy a bookshop with that'

I mull it over for a bit

I say, I guess you're pretty fucked then

He suggests we go on to another bar after dinner

I don't know this place at all

It's really noisy, some god-awful music is playing, so loud you can feel it in your bones

It's full of people half my age

I'm too old to be in a place like this

So is Kate, but she doesn't appreciate it when I point this out

Some guy bumps into me. He looks off his face on something

I tell her I'm going for a piss

When I come back Gerald's standing talking to her

I don't know how anyone can talk with this noise

It dawns on me while I'm watching them that Kate has slept with Gerald

The way they interact, her hand slightly touching his, him leaning in close, whispering in her ear

I go back to the bar to get us a drink, but when I turn around she's not there

I start wandering around, getting beer over my shirt

I don't feel in control

The music, and the people and…

When I find her she's still talking to him

I tell her we're going

I put down the drinks, I grab her arm

She tries to pull away and I take a firm grip of her hand

Gerald says something but I can't make it out

We head towards where I think the exit is

Somebody shouts something and I feel this hand in my back

The next thing I'm aware of is standing over some guy and I'm punching and I'm kicking him

Somebody pulls me away

The guy's just lying there on the floor

I guess his face looks pretty bad

It looks like he's been in a car accident or something

I don't think I could have done that to him though

I look around for Kate but I can't see her

I panic for a second

When I step outside the air hits me, I try to breathe

I see Kate running down the street and catch up to her

I take her hand and try to give her a kiss, but she turns away

I can see she's been crying

She can be a bit of a drama queen at times, I think

Although I guess it's my fault

I tell her to concentrate on her breathing, but she just
tells me to fuck off

I ask where Gerald went to but she doesn't answer

She says she wanted to have a nice evening and why do
I have to ruin everything

I know she expects an apology

I haven't been in a proper fight for years

It's not like me, really

I feel vigorous…young

On the way home Kate tells me she's pregnant

—

The police weren't clear about what'd happened

Although they didn't think there were any other cars
involved

It didn't make sense, they said

Maybe there'd been something in the road

Coming round the bend, I didn't see it

It was dark, late at night, raining

Maybe a deer had run out in front of us

I'd had a couple of drinks but nothing illegal

I was fit to drive

The car actually flipped over

It was a design flaw with that model

They've changed them now, I think

Given them a lower centre of gravity

They tell me I'm lucky to be alive

I don't feel lucky

I didn't even break any bones, just some cuts and bruises

I did have a blow to the head

I was in a coma for a few days

They don't think there's any permanent damage though

When I wake up I ask about Allison

And they tell me Allison has been killed

They'd fought to save her but there was nothing they could do

They said they were very sorry

I'm not sure what they had to be sorry about

They didn't kill her

—

After a few weeks I move into my new office

Or is it a broom cupboard

Six by five, I can barely get a desk in there

It is only temporary

It's mine though

I have almost seven hundred and fifty grand under management

Half of this is my own money

It's not enough

If I'm charging two and twenty, two per cent of three seven five is not enough to meet my overheads

It's not been as easy to get money as I'd hoped

People I thought were enthusiastic haven't come through and won't return my calls

I have a list of every person who was at my presentation

So I call every one of them, the American ones in the afternoon

There seems to be a lot of fear around, so no one wants to commit large sums

Towards the end of the day I reach Alex, of Long Term Capital

He apologises for not getting back to me, been busy, whatever, he tells me they're prepared to invest half a million

I'll have the funds month end

But that's it

No one else is interested and I can't understand why

——

When I get home Kate suggests we head off somewhere for the weekend

She's found this retreat she wants us to go on

A weekend of spiritual healing, specifically for couples it says on the website

In brackets underneath it says, 'price includes oneness blessing'

I have no idea what that is

I tell her I have too much work to do

She shows me some pictures of the place

It used to be a hotel, it overlooks a loch

It looks so peaceful something in me says yes

We arrive Friday at nearly midnight, go to our rooms

They don't even let couples share a room

They wake us at five

They have us do this, ah, couples meditation thing

I forget now what it's called

You sit opposite your partner

Look each other directly in the eye…

And that's it

You just keep looking into your partner's eyes

For one full hour

And you don't speak, and you try not to break your gaze, and…

I don't know

Something magical is supposed to happen

(Stares forward.)

… Kate's eyes are blue

I'm sure I knew that before, I must've known

I can only manage a few minutes before I find my eyes wandering

Looking around the room

All the loving couples

Gazing into each other's eyes

This was a mistake

I need to get out of here

I look back at Kate

Look at her face

I look down at her breasts, her stomach

She's starting to show a little

I try to imagine who might be in there

I try to picture the face of my unborn son

I reach over, put my hand on her stomach and I hold it there

Thinking maybe something profound will happen

Not sure what I'm expecting

That scene from *Alien*

But nothing bursts out of her

It all seems a bit mundane really

Not such a big deal after all

And in the grand scheme of things maybe it isn't

Except no one knows what the grand scheme of things is

At lunch they sit us all at these long wooden benches

Kate sits opposite

The guy on my right strikes up a conversation

I get a whiff of bad breath and stale sweat

I'd just like him to fuck off

He seems interested when I tell him what I do for a living

He was made redundant, put most of the money into stock

He's not doing too well, and wants my advice

Tells me some of the stuff he's been holding

Most of it's junk, blue-sky cancer cure kind of thing

Stocks with a good story

People flock to them

I tell him to ditch everything immediately and stay out of the markets, as he'll likely lose what money he has left

He thanks me and promises to do exactly that

But I know he won't

What he really wanted was for me to tell him he was right

And that everything would turn out alright

After dinner there's a ceremony for the oneness blessing

Everyone is invited

The oneness blessing giver is a short guy in his seventies

He has a long grey beard and long hair

I guess he looks a bit like Charles Manson, I thought he did

He says you can just watch if you prefer, you're not compelled to receive the blessing

But it would be 'advantageous' if you did

I'm not sure what that means but it sounds vaguely threatening

The blessing accelerates a change in consciousness, he says

I want to ask if there's any experimental evidence to confirm this but it seems inappropriate

There's some bell ringing and incense burning

Then everyone starts to go up

Kate nudges me

It seems more embarrassing to refuse than to go along

We wait in line

I suddenly feel like I'd rather be anywhere else than here

When I get to the front I kneel down in front of him

He places his hands on my head

All is one, he says

Be filled with the love of the universe

———

Monday morning in the office, six fifteen, I get a phone call

A guy I used to work beside, Greg

I've not spoken to him in a long while, years

I'm not even sure how he got my number, anyway he says he has a good deal for me

Free money, good as

It's an IPO, Amerita

He knows a guy at the NOMAD, had a tip, he's buying in himself

Advises me to do likewise

I tell him I'll think about it and get back to him

After I hang up I have this feeling like…a few months ago I wouldn't even have entertained thoughts like these - but is it possible I somehow caused him to call me?

I sent some kind of positive vibe or something out into the universe?

Is that possible? Or am I losing my fucking mind?

I call Greg straight back and tell him how much I'm in for, four hundred k, all told

I spend the rest of the morning going through every trade I've made

Getting married to certain positions is what kills you

The difference between winners and losers in this game is:

Winners know, when you're in a bad situation, just get out, take the hit, no matter how painful

Losers hold and hope

Money just used to be a way to keep score

Like a high score in a video game

That's all

But when it's my money at risk…

When a position goes bad, it's a knife in my gut

And every point it moves against me twists the knife, just a little

(Deep breath.)

I try to lean back in my chair, but my back needs to be straight to do this

I check the floor, don't think there's enough room

I push the terminal to one side, push everything to one side, climb up onto the desk

I sit cross legged on the desk, looking out on to the street and the offices opposite

Close my eyes

Feel the sun on my face

(Breathes in, calmly.) this is an in breath

(Breathes out.) this is an out breath

(Breathes in.)

(Breathes out.)

(Long pause.)

Shit!

I still need to paint the nursery

When I open my eyes I discover I have an audience

The people in the building opposite

They appear to be having a good laugh at my expense
and give me a round of applause as I awkwardly get up
and climb back down off the desk

I take a bow

And close the fucking blinds

——

Kate seems to want to spend less and less time with me

She's been helping Gerald with refurbishing the 'new' shop

He says she has a flair for design apparently

Can't say I've ever noticed

I'm either coming home to an empty house

Or she's there but there's nothing much to say

Or it's the baby this and when the baby is born that

She's excited about everything and can't understand why I'm not

When she starts talking about private schools it feels like she's goading me

I'll be flat broke long before then

We fight quite a lot I guess

It's not how it was

I'm spending fourteen hours a day in this office

A self-imposed solitary confinement

I've been sleeping in the office a few nights a week

Sitting alone in here seems less stressful than going home to her

The cleaners wake me up

I think, how did I create this situation?

How am I responsible?

Seven a.m., news comes over the wires that shares in Amerita have been suspended

Amerita is the company Greg pitched to me

One of the directors is to be investigated for fraud

I call looking for Greg, but he's stepped out

I call back and he's on a call

Eventually I call and he answers

I ask him what the story is

He's not exactly contrite

It happens, he says

He says he was burned as well but he's clearly lying

I want to throw the phone across the room but I don't

It's not even him I'm angry at

He didn't twist my arm

It was my decision

Every loser has a story

It's always someone else's fault

But every winner knows that's not true

You were sold a lie because you were looking to buy one

You're not a victim

You make yourself a victim

I spend the morning watching my last few positions

In two hours the Euro moves against me fourteen pips

Each pip's worth, what, fifteen hundred pounds?

Twenty-one thousand pounds of my money gone, in two hours

While I sit and watch it happen, because that's the game, it's nothing abnormal

But the nervous system wasn't evolved for the stock market

I'm sitting in an office watching a screen but my body's telling me my life is in danger

I'm being attacked

I ring around every broker I know, see if I can pick something up

Anything

No one seems to want to take my call

If I do get through, they're awkward, tell me they'll ring me back

Eventually I ask straight out what's going on

That's when I find out

Find out what John has been getting up to

Because I'm pursuing legal action against him, John has bad mouthed me to every client, fund manager, broker, every fucking person who might conceivably give me money or help

That's why I couldn't raise the money

So there is no more money

It's over

I'm finished

My phone rings

Kate

I answer

She says she's reading a book on kids' names that Gerald had given her, and what did I think of…

I don't know

I guess I don't really hear anything after that

———

Kate is upstairs when I get in

I can hear her talking to someone

I go into the kitchen, looking for something to eat, out of habit more than anything

When I go upstairs the shower's running

I sit on the bed and wait for her to come out

Her phone's on the night stand, I pick it up

The name isn't a surprise

I feel sick but there's also a kind of relief

Does that make sense?

She seems a bit startled when she opens the door and sees me sitting there

I ask her, how was work?

I ask her if she loves me

I ask her if she's had Gerald here, in our bed

I ask her if my son to be is really my son

I ask her – she turns to walk away

There's something else

Some…thing, there in the room with us

Observing

Something bearing witness

As Kate falls to the floor

Crying. Holding her stomach

Jesus. The fucking noise she's making

You'd think she was dying

She tells me to get out

Out of my own house

I go down the stairs and out the front door

I walk the streets

Everything looks odd

I don't know how long I walk for or where I go

——

By the time I get back to the house it's dark and the door's locked

I can't get in and I can't find my keys

I think maybe I left them in the back door

I climb over the garden fence, pick up this little stone figurine of a rabbit we have in the garden and I smash the window

When I get in, the house is quiet

The lights are on downstairs but I don't hear anything

Maybe she's gone

I call out but there's no answer

Check all the rooms downstairs, then go upstairs and go into the bedroom

The light's off but there's enough light from outside to see

There's a lot of blood on the floor

Think it's blood

I see Kate, lying there on the floor

At first I think she's dead

But I can hear her breathing

I don't know if she's in pain

I don't want her to suffer, I don't

Then I notice it

Just lying there

I can't see clearly what it is, but I know

I touch it with my foot

It doesn't move. How could it?

I feel trapped

Try to clear my head

To breathe

I sit on the bed

I sit there in the dark

I listen to Kate breathing

–

They'd asked me at the hospital if I wanted to talk to anyone about it

After the crash

About how I felt about Allison's death

No one blamed me but it was natural to feel guilty in these circumstances

And, 'was I feeling guilty?'

In truth, I didn't know what I felt

There didn't seem enough time

In the end I didn't talk to anyone about it and no one asked again

Allison's death was recorded as accidental

They had to have a closed casket

I couldn't even see her face again

Her parents were quite religious

I guess it brought some comfort to them

When I saw them her father hugged me and told me I mustn't torture myself

I wasn't responsible

He had so much kindness and compassion in his voice

I didn't say anything

Sometimes it's better to let people believe what they want to believe

He said he didn't know why this terrible thing had to happen

But there had to be a reason for it

Because there was a reason for everything

——

The markets continued to sell off overnight

The Asian markets break new lows for the year

The Footsie opens down over a hundred points

CNBC is on in the corner

They mention Barclays as a potential bidder for Lehman

Then they start talking about the wider market reaction

One of the talking heads says there is the potential for unprecedented volatility

Which is a stupid thing to say

Not because it's not true

But because it's always true

I watch some of my open positions go from red, to blue

The half million from Long Term Capital is in my account

It's around lunch time when they turn up at the office

They have some news for me and would I please sit down

It's the older one who says this

The other officer doesn't say anything

I wonder if he's watching to see how I react

To see if I look surprised

Your partner Kate has been murdered, he says

He explains what happened

How many times she'd been stabbed

I don't know if he expects me to say anything

I stare at the floor

She was pregnant I say to them

I'm not sure why I say that, what the fuck difference does
it make?

They ask me if I can come down to the station with
them, to answer some questions

Just routine stuff

They give me a few minutes alone

At the station they ask me if Kate and I had been getting on

They keep asking

I don't ask for a lawyer even though I'm entitled

They want to know where I was

I tell them I was in the office

I tell them to speak to the cleaners at the office

They would vouch for me being there

Eventually they let me go

—

The next few weeks in the markets are crazy

It's like nothing I've ever seen

Nothing anyone has seen

There's 'unprecedented volatility'

It feels kind of…historic

It feels like the end

But it's not

In two weeks I make more money than the average person will in ten years

Some people make <u>things</u>

I make money, and I'm fucking good at it

Why should I be ashamed of that?

I hear the car before I see it

The same two guys

The older policeman asks if they can come in for a few minutes

He says they have a suspect

There'd been robberies in the area

A similar incident had occurred a few months before

They think Kate interrupted them in the act

They have a guy in custody, they're confident it was him

That's the story they've come up with anyway

The younger policeman says they'll do their best to make sure he goes to prison for a long time

If it's any consolation

I thank them

As they're leaving the older one says he's very sorry

Kate's mother has flown back from New Zealand for the funeral

It's busier than I would have expected

I didn't realise she knew so many people

I recognise a few of them from the meditation class

Toby's here as well

They've asked him to do a reading

He likens Kate's life to a wave in the ocean

He says, our separation from her now, is an illusion

Because our separation from each other is an illusion

Afterwards I go for a walk in the park

Find an empty bench and watch the ducks

Everything looks very bright for some reason

I've never noticed how beautiful this place is

There's a woman passing by, pushing a kid in a stroller

She has lovely, long blonde hair

Her kid looks up at me, smiling

I meet his gaze

For a second I let myself imagine bringing my son here

Kicking a ball around

Giving him some bread to feed the ducks

I start to cry, sitting there in the park

The woman stops, and asks me if I'm alright

I say

I don't know

I don't know anything

——

END OF PLAY

WWW.OBERONBOOKS.COM